My mom fi th
me, helping m th
me. Llamas: you have my heart. Women of TNMP, thank you for teaching me what fearless writing looks and sounds and feels like. Many people cared for my kids so I could hide myself away and write, including Akirah, Winkie, and especially Sandy—thank you! This book would not exist without my deep, gifted, loving friend and editor, Christianne.

My extended family, thank you for teaching me about how a family should love. To Aunt Mary Beth, who couldn't wait to read this book and didn't get to, I love you and miss you. Anything I know about parenting well I learned from my parents. Mom, thank you for teaching me how to listen, how to be strong, and how to care for others. Dad, thank you for showing me how to hear and follow the Holy Spirit. My brother and sister are my best and closest companions. I feel ridiculously lucky to have siblings who really are my best friends. My kids take me to the place beyond words, and every page of this is a love letter to them. And finally, Nick—how did I get so lucky? Sharing life with you is the best, and I still can't believe I get to be your wife.

My life is full of love, and I am deeply grateful.

INTRODUCTION

The most beautiful word on the lips of [humankind] is the word "Mother," and the most beautiful call is the call of "My mother." It is a word full of hope and love, a sweet and kind word coming from the depths of the heart.

—Kahlil Gibran[1]

"What does it look like to pursue holiness as a mother?" I asked my journal. It was September 2011, and my oldest son was about to turn one. His two siblings were yet to be born. I was a year into motherhood, and every day I felt like I was barely keeping my head above water. My life was diapers and feedings and sleepless nights after diapers and feedings and sleepless nights. In the whirlwind of these physical demands, I struggled to find time for myself, let alone time for God.

In the stolen moments I found to consider the question of holiness in motherhood, all I could picture was an angel floating on a cloud bouncing a baby on her knee. This image was absurd and unattainable. The next image that came to mind was Mary, serene and Sphinx-like as she treasured all she experienced in her heart—also unattainable. I realized that any picture I had for holiness in motherhood did not match my own messy, challenging reality. I missed the deep relationship with God that I had cultivated through prayer and journaling, retreats and service. I feared I would never have that close relationship with the Lord again.

I also feared that now mothering would be my only path of relationship with God. I was wary of any suggestion that motherhood reveals the true holy path for women. I didn't want all of who I was in God to be reduced to motherhood. I rejected the notion that we are made whole or complete through becoming a mother, as if something is lacking in us that can only be filled by children. God's creativity and imagination are greater than that. Yet I couldn't escape that lingering sense of curiosity, that question of what holiness in motherhood could be like. What if motherhood could be a spiritual practice?

Part of my curiosity, when I wrote that question, came from my work as a spiritual director. I began my training in spiritual direction the year Declan, my oldest, was born. Spiritual direction is a practice of listening for the presence of God in your life. Spiritual directors meet with individuals or groups. Directees share what is happening in their life, the good and the bad, and together with their director, they explore where and how God might be moving and what invitations God might be offering. The goal is to grow deeper in relationship with God based on the belief that God is active wherever we are active.

As a new mother and an emerging spiritual director, I wondered how to integrate my passions—to bring my spiritual self into my life as a mom. Life was hectic and I was just getting by, so this question lay dormant for three years. I birthed two more babies, completed my training, and began to work as a spiritual director. When that seed of a question finally sprouted, it sprang up as a fully formed idea: a book that would invite mothers to explore the spiritual journey of motherhood.

It happened at the tail end of a conference I attended in Louisville, Kentucky, in 2015 with Spiritual Directors International. This organization hosts a gathering of spiritual companions each year that refreshes and inspires me, both professionally and personally. I was invited to serve that year as the facilitator for the New Contemplatives Initiative, which offers scholarships to involve more young spiritual directors in the organization. In my role, I helped a talented group of younger directors build community with one another and with the wider community. I also helped them prepare a presentation that allowed them to share their collective wisdom with the conference attendees.

During this year's conference, six of my friends—all of whom are young spiritual directors living in different places around the world—came to Pittsburgh, where I live, so we could drive to Louisville together. My daughter, Healy, was just three months old, and she traveled with us. With her car seat nestled in the center of the van, my friend Nita called her the "heartbeat of our caravan."

On the drive back to Pittsburgh after the conference, I asked my friends, "What invitation are you hearing out of this time?" For the next six hours, each of them described the deep soul connections they had made, the inspiring conversations in which they had participated, the seeds of ideas that were planted over the weekend, and the ways they could imagine those seeds coming to life when they returned home.

I listened in awe and gratitude—and in jealousy. I had spent much of the conference rushing between my baby and the group of New Contemplatives. I nursed between presentations and rocked Healy in the back of the room during workshops. My parents met us at the conference and helped with her while I worked with the New Contemplatives, but even when Healy wasn't with me, she was on my mind.

In the van on that drive back, the conversation eventually slowed. Then my friend Lance asked, "What about you, Lauren?"

I started to cry. I told them how different my experience had been from theirs, how shrouded in motherhood it had been.

"I would like to have big dreams," I told them, "but I can't think beyond wanting sleep and oxygen—space to breathe."

"What if you *did* have a big dream?" he asked. "What would it be?"

"It would be to write a book," I said.

I was surprised by these words. My desire to write had lain dormant for so long, hibernating beneath the demanding day-to-day reality of life with my kids. I had forgotten how to listen for and hear my own deep longings.

But there it was: I wanted to write a book. And I knew exactly what type of book it would be. It would be a book that honored the mess and the fatigue and the frustrations of our daily lives as mothers, as well as its joys. It would be a book that explored the holiness of motherhood and brought my curiosity as a spiritual director to bear on my experience as a mom. It would be the book I'd wished I'd had when I became a mother and that I still need as I navigate life with my three children today and wonder how God is present through it all. It would be this book.

The Spiritual Directors International conference in Louisville took place during the 100th anniversary of Thomas Merton's birth. Merton was a Trappist monk, a mystic and poet, and an activist. A prolific author, his books on spirituality have shaped the face of contemporary Christianity. Much of the 2015 conference was centered on his life and work. As part of the festivities, we were invited to make a pilgrimage to Fourth and Walnut, an important location in Merton's life. It was there, at a busy city street corner, that Merton had a famous epiphany he relays in his book *Conjectures of a Guilty Bystander*:

In Louisville, at the corner of Fourth and Walnut, in the center of the shopping district, I was suddenly overwhelmed with the realization that I loved all those people, that they were mine and I theirs, that we could not be alien to one another even though we were total strangers. It was like waking from a dream of separateness. . . . And if only everybody could realize this! But it cannot be explained. There is no way of telling people that they are all walking around shining like the sun.[2]

Merton witnessed the beauty and holiness that dwells within each person and experienced a profound sense of interconnectedness. Fourth and Walnut has become a place of pilgrimage, where pilgrims honor Merton's memory and look for their own experience of God shining in everyone around them. As part of the conference, we were given ribbons to tie around the plaque that commemorates this sacred spot in the center of downtown Louisville. It was a way to connect with the spirit of Thomas Merton, to connect with the community of spiritual directors, and to remember that the work of spiritual direction is the work of seeing and honoring the unique ways we each shine forth the glory of God.

As the days of the conference passed, I heard story after story from other attendees of how meaningful it was for them to visit Fourth and Walnut. Meanwhile, my ribbon still lay in my bag, and I had no hope of finding time to tie it around the plaque. I was frustrated to not get to participate in this collective holy moment. As I nursed my daughter and prayed through the disappointment, God spoke to me: *This is not your pilgrimage. Your pilgrimage is your journey back home.*

When I got home, I tied the ribbon that was intended for Fourth and Walnut around a lamp in my living room and thanked God for the way the people in my house shine like the sun. That ribbon has served as a visual reminder to tune in to the beauty and holiness of my family. It reminds me to pause from the mundane and open my eyes to the divine.

The invitation to make a pilgrimage to my own home showed me that I had been asking the wrong question. It's not about whether motherhood is a better way to connect with God or a worse way, a holier or less holy path. It simply is my path, and God desires to meet me on it. The Lord wasn't hanging out at that Louisville street corner, wondering when I would show up. God meets me within this life. God desires to meet you in your life as well. The spiritual life is not found only on Sundays, or on a mountain peak, or in the Bible, or at Fourth and Walnut. It didn't die when we had children or go into hibernation until our kids get older. It is now, here: This life is the spiritual life. Our pilgrimage begins wherever we are.

This life where God desires to meet me is not mine alone. My life ceased belonging to me when I became a mom: My time was no longer mine, my body was no longer mine, no part of my day belonged to me alone. It was a difficult reality to adjust to, but I also suspect it always has been true—my life was never just my own. My children have invited me into a deeper reality. My life was always shared with God, who continually draws me into closer relationship with God's self and with others. My children have broken me of the false narrative of my life being my own. I now know that it belongs to God, to my partner, to my children, and to my community as well as to myself.

This sharing of life, this "ours" instead of "mine," is not all sacrifice and hardship. With collective identity comes life-giving connection and belonging. One of the most beautiful pieces of shared life has been in my friendships with other mothers. For each of us, becoming a mother meant crossing a profound threshold. Life is different on the other side. I am grateful for the sisterhood of connection that is woven of our shared experiences. Likewise, I share my motherhood with you, knowing that we are connected through the path of parenting. I hope this book will be a place of relationship, a place to share life with each other and with God, a place to remember that you are not alone.

If this life that is ours is the spiritual life, if God desires to meet us within our parenting, how can we experience that? Perhaps we could each begin our exploration with a ribbon, with a way to name our homes and lives as holy ground. These pages will help you continue the journey. They will be a light on the path as we practice encountering God and encountering our true selves within the chaotic choreography of motherhood.

As a spiritual director, I have the privilege of hearing people's stories. I bear witness to the ways God reaches out to my directees and the ways they respond. I watch the relationship unfold between them and God.

There are patterns to these stories, and similar themes: love, loss, consolation, desolation, joy, grief. But the way these themes unfold in a person's life and the way God speaks to them and they respond are always original. We are each unique, and it is one of my greatest joys to be present to the myriad mysterious ways the Lord moves in each life that I companion.

Motherhood holds that same tension. Shared patterns overlay each individual experience. We share the experience of dying to our egos, of falling in love with our children, of feeling like we can't do it, and of being made new ourselves. Yet we each live out our motherhood and hear the Holy Spirit's whispers in our unique way.

There is no obvious way to be present to the spirituality of parenting, to attend to Christ in your children and your own deepening in holiness. Your way is not my way, and how you grow and connect today will be different from how you grow and connect tomorrow. I hope my companionship keeps you focused on your path and encourages you in your efforts. I will wonder with you about the places to explore next and what it means to be where you are.

After a period of **Preparation Days**, our exploration of this holy life will unfold in three parts. In the first, **Becoming a Mother**, we will return to the memories of first crossing the threshold of motherhood. We will look honestly at our experiences, the places of consolation and desolation, the points of light and darkness. We will hold these memories gently and listen for God's voice within them. We then move to **Becoming Yourself** to reflect on the ways our own identities are forged alongside our children's. This section is an invitation to come home to yourself as you listen for who God is creating you to be. The third section, **Becoming Holy**, considers some of the ways mothering draws us deeper into life with God. It honors the ways mothering is holy work.

In each reflection, I share a bit of my journey and then ask questions that invite you to explore your own story. I hope the questions will be spaces of opening and expansion for you, that they will help you create time to sit with your experience and listen to your life. You could move through this book in a daily rhythm, reading a reflection every day. You could move more slowly, staying with each reflection for several days or a week. You could read the book in order, maybe using a ribbon as a bookmark, or you could flip to sections at random. Move at the pace that is right for you. Choosing your pace for the book can be your first step in this practice of listening to your life as you listen for your own needs and desires as well as God's invitation within the pages.

Use this book as it works for you. Some of the reflections and questions in this book may not engage you, and that is fine. Other questions may contain worlds for you to explore. If certain questions are surprising or uncomfortable or full of solace, stay with them. Bring the question to God in prayer and ask what God might want to reveal to you. Stay with the question, repeating your reading and reflection, for as long as you feel led.

I hope you find a way to share your responses to the reflection questions, the holy moments you experience, the stories that are yours. You might carry the questions through the day with you and answer them in your heart. You might journal your responses. You might talk about your thoughts and experiences with your partner, a close friend, or in prayer with God. You might use this book to guide discussion in your community or with a small group. You might find it fruitful to work through these questions with a spiritual director. However you process your engagement with this book, I pray that it opens a window to your soul.

This book creates space for you—the beautiful, unique mother you are to your beautiful, unique children—to contemplate your relationship with your children and your relationship with God; to rest, to mourn, to be in awe, and to experience the presence of the holy in the mundane. May these pages be a companion as you awaken to the holy potential of this life that is ours.

PREPARATION DAYS

Several years ago, I began praying through something called the Ignatian Spiritual Exercises. It is a school of discipleship, a "retreat" you can make in your daily life to draw closer to God, and I couldn't wait to get started. I committed to praying for an hour a day for however long it would take to complete the Exercises—at least six months.

The Exercises were written by Ignatius of Loyola in the early 1500s, and they are divided into four "weeks." I was surprised, then, that I didn't start my Exercises with Week One. Instead, my spiritual director guided me through Ignatius's "Preparation Days," prayers that were meant to open my heart to what was coming and that would provide guidance for learning the Ignatian forms of prayer.

My eager heart felt frustrated by this slower start to the process at the time, but I've now come to see its wisdom. Preparation Days are like a base camp, a place to anticipate what is coming and to practice gently some of the skills we will need to walk the journey.

In this preliminary section, I would like to offer the same to you. Here, we are going to consider some steps you can take to prepare to enter this holy journey into the heart of your life as a mother.

Physical Space

First, let's consider the place you might go to pray with these reflections. Where in your house could you sit regularly to read and ponder and pray? Even if you're only able to carve out a few minutes to reflect, it can be helpful to have a regular place for it—a spot that is yours. You could light a candle to mark your entrance into prayer. You could place a picture, icon, or painting nearby that speaks to you in some way of God's love. You could keep a cozy blanket in that spot to wrap around yourself to remind you that you are held and loved by God.

I wrote most of this book at a small table in our guest room. It is far from glamorous. A folding chair sits at my first kitchen table, which I bought from IKEA when I was in college. I keep an electric blanket nearby to tuck around my legs on cold days. On the wall hangs a painting of a grey wagtail surrounded by vibrant flowers that was painted by my talented friend Claire; it invites me to explore the beautiful wilds. On the table, nestled amid stacks of books and papers, rests a small statue of Mary cradling an infant Jesus. I light a candle before I pick up my pen to remind me that writing is prayer.

Your space doesn't have to be perfect or clean or set aside just for prayer. It could be your favorite spot on the couch or a chair at the kitchen table amid the dirty dinner dishes. I have different spots in different rooms for different activities or times of day. I place a pillow against the wall when I pray in the guest room. In the living room, I curl up on the couch with spiritual reading and my morning coffee. My friend Amber, a fellow mother, has set up a prayer space in her dark, unfinished basement. It's not beautiful, she says, but it is quiet and private.

In his Spiritual Exercises, Saint Ignatius considers preparation for prayer to be nearly as important as prayer itself. He instructs retreatants to stand before their prayer space before they settle into prayer and to pray an Our Father to prepare their hearts and mark the transition. You could try the same, pausing for a moment to center yourself before physically settling in to your chosen space. Wherever your reading and prayer space may be, try to find a place where you can cross a physical or metaphorical threshold as you approach the space to read, to wonder, and to pray.

> *Where in your house could be your holy place?*
> *How will you mark your entrance into prayer?*

Interior Space

In addition to preparing a physical place to pray, I invite you to prepare a place within, an interior space in which to meet yourself and to meet God.

To help you create this space, first take some time to remember where and when you have felt most loved, most at home, and most peaceful. Savor these memories and the emotions they stir in you. What elements from those spaces can inspire your interior space? My spiritual director loves the ocean, and she often imagines she is at the beach when she prays. I know someone whose interior space resembles a dark, quiet cave. I often picture myself sitting with Jesus at a campfire, where we rest and share stories.

In *Practicing the Presence of God,* Brother Lawrence describes the heart as a prayer room, a place to encounter God. The heart is also a place to encounter ourselves. By imagining this place, we practice interior hospitality. We create room within our heart to receive ourselves and to explore our journey with "the kindness and reverence of candlelight," as the poet and philosopher John O'Donohue writes.[1] I invite you to create a space within your heart where you can meet God. May it be a sanctuary where you can bring your new, tender self to be held in warmth and light.

> *What image or feeling helps you imagine such a place within you? How might that space help you to explore your experience as a mother and ponder where God has been present to you?*

Practicing Contemplation

Preparation Days are an opportunity to try on a posture of contemplation, which theologian Walter Burghardt, SJ, defines as "a long, loving look at the real."[2] To practice contemplation is to practice being a bit more awake to our days in a way that frees us from judgment and opens our hearts to others. Contemplation is closely related to mindfulness, the practice of grounding yourself in the present moment, no matter where you are or what you are doing. It is being present as you change pee-soaked sheets, sweep up spilled or thrown food, and take in the warmth of your child as she hugs your legs mid-task. As a mom, opening up to contemplation is both challenging and freeing. It provides a momentary release from the running narrative of all there is to do and all the ways it can be done better. It opens us to the gift of this very moment.

Here is a way to practice: Take a few minutes to notice how your body is feeling. Are you hot, cold, tired, sore, hungry? Where in your body do you experience pain or discomfort? As you notice how your physical body is feeling, check in with your soul as well. What emotions do you feel in this moment? What thoughts circle your mind? What worries for your family or the world weigh on your heart? As you notice the things that weigh on your body and soul, gently release them without judgment.

You can practice being contemplative throughout the day by taking a moment to identify your physical state and emotions and by taking a few deep and centering breaths. I call these moments "contemplative pauses," tiny breaks in my day when I detach from the chaos around me and center myself within the deeper reality of God's love. You can practice spontaneously throughout the day or set a reminder on your phone to invite you into a contemplative pause. Growing in awareness of how you are, who you are, and what you are experiencing will be a central part of our journey.

What does contemplation mean to you? As you begin to practice pausing within your day, what do you notice?

Practicing Silence

God can communicate with us through any moment in our life. God can reach out to us through our emotions, our physical senses, or a feeling of weight or lightness of being. God can speak to us through the words of a friend or words on a page; through music, nature, and our children. But God seems to be particularly drawn to silence and subtlety. In 1 Kings 19:11-12 (NIV), the Lord tells Elijah to stand on the mountain and wait, as the Lord is about to pass by:

> A great and powerful wind tore the mountains apart and shattered the rocks before the LORD, but the LORD was not in the wind. After the wind there was an earthquake, but the LORD was not in the earthquake. After the earthquake came a fire, but the LORD was not in the fire. And after the fire came a gentle whisper.

The Lord, as God so often is, was in the whisper, in the gentleness, in the quiet instead of the chaos.

I find God's preference for silence challenging and often incompatible with my life as a mother. God may be in the silence, but my children are in the powerful wind, the earthquake, and the fire. Life with children is loud and chaotic.

So many things call for our attention. When I finally meet silence, I often don't know what to do with it. I'm out of practice, and I forget how to sit and breathe, in and out, and to leave space for the Lord to speak.

I know God doesn't only communicate in the silence. I believe God speaks to us through the whole of our life. But silence creates space for us to practice listening for God so that we may better experience God's presence in all areas. Silence is a spiritual practice that prepares us to receive mothering as a spiritual practice. It is a practice I need help practicing.

I invite you to practice being in silence. You could start with this: Set a timer for just five minutes. For those five minutes, pick one focal point. It could be your breath. It could be your heartbeat. It could be an image of Jesus, either physical or imagined. You could try a single word. Pick one thing, and then let the timer run. Let yourself feel uncomfortable. Let your mind wander, and then gently bring it back to your point of focus. Then, when the timer goes off, you're done. Don't worry about how it went or if it was a "good" or "bad" time of silence. Remind yourself that this is practice.

Are you naturally drawn to quiet, or is this a more challenging practice for you? As you practice sitting in silence, what do you notice? What bubbles to the surface?

Stay with the practice of daily silence and contemplation, and the other reflections of these Preparation Days, as long as you wish. Move forward when you feel ready, whether that's in a day, a week, or a month.

Lastly, I offer a blessing for you, as you begin the journey:

May courage be yours.
May peace be yours.
May patience and curiosity and wonder be yours.
May you be met with ample space to hold your
    own story.
May each period mark a holy pause and a deep
    breath.
May you stay with your thoughts,
Dance with your imagination,
And follow the nudging of the Spirit.
May the words be here when you need them
And fall away when you don't.
May the path lead you home to yourself again.
May the road wind you deeper into the heart of
    God.
Amen.

PART I
Becoming a Mother

The First Moments

Before my first son was born, I had two miscarriages. Those losses were both physically and emotionally painful, and I doubted I would ever become a mother. My mom and my friends told me I was already a mother to the two babies I had lost, but that didn't feel real at the time. During my third pregnancy, doubt and fear crowded out my hope. Since I had lost so much already, I found it hard to believe this child would ever live outside of my womb.

When I was a week past my due date, Nick and I went in for a routine ultrasound to make sure the baby was still healthy and safe. Midway through, the tech paused the ultrasound, called the midwife on duty, and then put me on the phone with her.

"Your amniotic fluid is low," the midwife said. "It is time for you to have this baby."

So much began to swirl through my heart and mind. I felt joy that it was time. At forty-one weeks, I had begun to feel I would be pregnant forever. I felt fear and sadness too as this meant I would need to be induced, rather than having the completely natural childbirth I had planned. I also felt panic. We were unprepared for this moment; we had not brought our bag to the hospital (a rookie mistake!). I hadn't made our bed or eaten breakfast. I was not ready.

The midwife gave us permission to go home and get the bag, so long as we promised to be back within an hour. I moved through that hour in a fog of nervous excitement. We rushed to Panera, where I ate a bagel as quickly as I could. At home, I threw the comforter over our bed and crammed last-minute items into the hospital bag.

Then we were back to the hospital in the birthing room, where Nick taped soothing pictures of the ocean and fall leaves to the walls and turned on our CD of ocean sounds. My doula and my parents were on their way. I was given something to soften my cervix and told to rest and relax.

"Most women don't feel a thing right now," the nurse said, "although 5 percent of women do experience strong contractions." I was in the 5 percent. I went from feeling nothing to having intense, painful contractions every two minutes. I couldn't catch my breath or get ahead of them. I started vomiting and couldn't stop, so I asked for an epidural.

"Are you *sure* this is what you want?" the midwife asked. "Your birth plan says we should try to talk you out of it."

Through waves of nausea and pain, I managed to say, "Nothing about this was in the plan!"

I got the epidural at 5:00 p.m., six hours after we'd arrived for the induction.

It was a long, slow night of waiting for my body to be ready to birth. At 1:00 a.m., when everyone in the room except me and my doula had slept, the nurse said I was ready to push. Four hours later—an absurd, surreal amount of time to have spent pushing—my body figured out what to do. I could feel the "ring of fire" as Declan's head crowned.

Push and push and push—his head was out. Push. *Push*.

His tiny body slipped free of mine, and he was *here*, sliding around on my belly as I wrapped my shaking arms around him. He was the most stunning thing I had ever seen. I repeated in a chant of wonder, "He's here. He's real. I can't believe it. He's perfect. He's beautiful. I can't believe he's here."

At first, the midwife seemed pleased with how he was doing. Then a shadow of concern crossed her face. She held him and smacked his bottom once, then twice. He gave a small yelp, as if to say, "I'm just fine, but if you need me to make a sound, I will."

I could feel the deep peace of Declan's personality already present. I was in total awe of him, of myself, of the moment, and of the paradigm shift his birth brought to me. I seemed to feel reality rupture and rebuild itself in that moment: life before and life after.

Tell Your Story

Remember your first birth story or the first time you met your first child through adoption, fostering, or stepmothering. What did those first moments of becoming a mother hold for you?

The First Days

Declan's birth overwhelmed me with its holiness. And it overwhelmed me with pain. I was exhausted, I could barely stand, and all I wanted was sleep. I had just done the most challenging physical thing I had ever done, by far, and it seemed I should get time to recover.

Instead, my focus immediately went to another physical being. I nursed fifteen to twenty minutes per side every two hours, praying my milk would come in. I bathed and changed my newborn and greeted visitors who came to see me in my hospital room. My broken body felt like an afterthought to me, my visitors, and the hospital staff as Declan drew the attention of everyone in the room. Through the dense fog of exhaustion and recovery, I wondered when I would feel the joy, when I would stop feeling like I was operating beyond my capacity.

After we left the hospital and went home, I couldn't sleep. My body had trained itself to hear every snuffle and whimper and snort of the newly breathing being beside me.

I urged my body to relax, but my knowing I had only an hour until the next feeding kept me awake.

My anxiety and physical fatigue worsened. Thankfully, after about a week, my mother took charge: "The baby is not sleeping in your room tonight, and I'm giving him a bottle." I slept for a blessed four-hour stretch that night. I realized that I would have to learn how to take care of myself too if I were going to make it through this season. Declan wasn't the only one who needed to sleep, to eat, and to be bathed. I needed to care for my physical self with meals and showers and rest.

That small stretch of sleep gave me a tiny bit of distance, which helped me to see Declan and to take in his beauty. He would blink at me with his large, blue eyes, and everything else in my world would fall away like dust compared to the sheer miracle of his peaceful, perfect being. Finally, I felt something other than fear and fatigue. I felt love, deep and all-encompassing and new.

Tell Your Story

As you reflect on those first days of motherhood, what do you notice? How did you respond to this life-altering shift?

The First Months

Iwas intensely lonely when I first became a mother. The days felt long and monotonous. I had friends I sometimes saw and even friends who lived with us. But that occasional companionship was no match for the length of the days, the shortness of my fuse when my son wouldn't nap, and the isolation I felt when I couldn't figure out how to get time to shower and when the idea of dressing myself in real clothes and feeding myself real food felt impossible. I was overwhelmed.

My husband tried to help, but it felt like we were living on different planets. He ate a hot breakfast, put on dress clothes, and left the house—every day. At work, he had conversations with other adults. He worked hard, and his bosses recognized his efforts and praised his work. I longed for that kind of visibility and acknowledgment and reassurance.

The differences between my world and Nick's didn't stop there. Beyond being appreciated and treated like an adult, when he had to go to the bathroom, *he just went*. Can you imagine? And if he wanted a cup of coffee, he got himself one and drank it—while it was still hot. Then, when he was hungry, he would eat. Can you imagine the luxury of that? I couldn't. Not anymore.

While I did a lot of internal work on not resenting how easy his life seemed and focusing on being grateful for his job and for our home and shared life together, I didn't know how to change my sense of isolation and loneliness.

My strongest memory from that early season of mothering is the swirling sense of disorientation as I lived through the 24/7 demands of caring for and loving my baby. Every tiny milestone, from the first successful breastfeeding latch to his first coos and laughs, felt like a miracle. I knew I was on holy ground; yet I couldn't put down roots there. The moments seemed to slip through my fingers because I no longer knew who I was. I had lost my identity. The self bearing witness to those miracles couldn't hold on to them. I had no framework through which to process my experience. Only now, seven years later, am I grounded enough in myself to return to those memories and savor them more deeply.

Tell Your Story

What sacrifices did new motherhood ask of you? How did you find yourself responding? How was it with your soul in those early days?

Ego Deaths

Before having kids, I thrived on praise—my love lan-
guage is words of affirmation. I want to do a good job, I
work hard to do a good job, and I need to hear from someone
else that I have done a good job for it to seem true. Those
first months of parenting were a kind of torture in this sense.
Here I was, working harder and giving more of myself than
ever before to something completely new and unknown, and
I received no feedback. I felt like I was flailing in the dark,
stumbling down an unknown path with nothing guiding me.

Oh, I would get *advice*. People would say, "It will be
so much easier for you if you co-sleep," while others said,
"Whatever you do, don't co-sleep!" Or "Make sure you start
him on a bottle early or he'll never take one," while others
advised, "Don't start on a bottle too soon; you don't want
nipple confusion!" These conflicting words left me with the
sense that I would never get it right. No one offered the affirmation I longed for, the words I most needed to hear: "Lauren, it was really beautiful the way you walked with Declan

in the living room for three hours to comfort him while he was teething. You knew exactly what he needed. You're really good at this whole mom thing!" I felt painfully invisible.

In *The Spiritual Child*, Lisa Miller describes parenthood as an ego death: "Parenting is an erosion of vanity and of the illusion of control."[1] Oh, how hard a time my ego has had with motherhood! I have experienced ego death through invisibility, the death of never feeling seen. I have not invited the death, allowed it to come gracefully, or taken it lightly. I have hated the lack of feedback that comes from interacting with others. My ego's death struggled hard to have its way with me.

Today, years into the adventure of parenting, I mostly feel peace with that ego death. I feel freedom in my days with my kids and comfortable in who I am with them. I no longer yearn for someone else to tell me how I am doing— which isn't to say I have figured out everything, just that I've had more practice.

I can see the graces of releasing the image of myself I encounter through others. The shadow side of longing to be seen is caring too much about what other people think and putting too much stock in others' opinions. I always followed what felt like the "right path," using success and adventure and the good opinions of others as my decision criteria. By completely stepping off a career trajectory and no longer receiving feedback related to my work, I realized the career path I was following was no longer joyful. In the hours of silence with my newborn, I began to feel new desires for a different kind of work that honored my love of story and journey and Jesus. I don't know that I would have been able to recognize and respond to God's invitation to become a spiritual director without this ego death. Like writing, spiritual direction is often quiet, hidden work. In letting go of my former self-image, I could make space for a new and truer me to be born.

Tell Your Story

What ego deaths did you experience upon becoming a mother? What have you lost that you might need to make space to mourn? Have you yet witnessed anything new being born from these deaths?

Easier Deaths

Like many women, I have agonized over my appearance. I have wished my hair were less frizzy and my skin less pale. I didn't like wearing shorts because of the cellulite on my thighs, and I wouldn't wear white shirts because they might show sweat. I wanted to be seen, but I didn't want anyone to look at me too closely. I saved the brunt of my scorn for my hips, which seemed to be absurdly wide, no matter how much I exercised or how carefully I ate. I hated swimsuits and tight skirts and anything else that drew attention to them.

Then I had a baby. And another and another. I haven't thought about my hips in years, at least not in a cosmetic sense. I just don't care anymore. I still like to wear nice clothes, and I still wear a little bit of makeup, but I cannot tell you the last time I worried about the appearance of my body.

This death snuck up and surprised me. It is one I hadn't thought to ask for but that I embrace with open arms. It is so freeing not to care about how I look. My lack of caring is born of my body no longer being my own. When Declan was small, he was permanently attached to me, altering my center of gravity and blurring the lines between where his body ended and my body began. Now, when I cross the street with my three children, two hold hands and the third grabs my coat, and we awkwardly bumble across the street like some strange four-headed being—and that feels like reality. I am part of a larger organism. The irony is that in becoming less independent in my body, I am more independent in my spirit. Although I've never had someone as intimately connected to me as my children, I feel freer than I ever have before. I am both more dependent and more independent than I have ever been.

This is a death that feels like freedom. It is the death of self-consciousness.

Tell Your Story

In your experience of motherhood, are there deaths you celebrate, losses that surprise you, changes you haven't sought out but that make you sing for joy?

Life from Death

When I became a mother, my identity—all the pieces of me that make up my personality, my personal narrative, my sense of who I am—got swept up into the swirling chaos of life with a newborn. I felt like a tornado had torn through me and upended every part of myself. Although I wanted to search for the dislocated pieces of myself, I first had to find my bearings. Before I could come back home to myself, I first had to find my home within motherhood. In part, I had to find a home in motherhood as a matter of physical survival: My baby needed to eat every three hours, and I needed to be the one to feed him. But it was also a spiritual reality. I had tumbled across the threshold of motherhood, and I needed to locate myself in this new land.

I met the mother in me when I gazed at my son in wonder, when I winced and readjusted his body after a painful breastfeeding latch, and when I breathed in his powdery scent. I saw my capacity for love stretch beyond recognition as one sleepless night bled into a restless day and another sleepless night. As I interacted with my son and reordered my daily existence around his needs, I found that I was more playful than I expected and more easily irritated than I would have hoped. I lost the sense of self I received from others, but I saw a new version of myself reflected in Declan's early smiles. I began to realize I didn't need others to tell me I was doing a good job. I could affirm it for myself.

I finally learned that I was not caring for this child alone. I knew our circle of love, which included Nick, our parents and siblings, our extended families, and all our friends, was in the dance of life with us. I realized that I could mother my child within that circle of support. I stopped thinking, *I don't know if I can do this. I don't know if I'm ready to be a mother.* I realized I was capable.

In meeting myself as a mother, I found solid ground. The swirl calmed as the days settled into a rhythm. My mind began to quiet, to relax into new patterns, and I stopped worrying, *Has he slept too long? Has he eaten enough? What should we do next? When will we do tummy time?* As I took my first solid steps into the land of motherhood and eased out of that initial panicked whirlwind, I began to come home to myself.

Tell Your Story

How did you meet yourself as a mother in those early days? How did you surprise yourself? When did you find yourself within your mothering?

Beholding Beauty

When Declan was first placed in my arms after birth, I said again and again, in awe and physical shock, "He's beautiful. He's beautiful. He's beautiful." These beings entrusted to us are breathtaking. Yet to be awake to this beauty is exhausting. Beholding their beauty can shatter our senses. In her book *In the Sanctuary of Women*, Jan Richardson ponders Eve and the beauty of beholding another person fully by asking, "What if it wasn't their shame that drove them to garb themselves but rather their beauty? What if seeing each other with eyes wide open was too overwhelming to bear? To fully see and be seen is dazzling."[1]

Our children are dazzlingly, painfully beautiful. Their beauty can be overwhelming. And while it can be hard to find moments to break away from the busyness of each day and let the fullness of their beauty sink in, perhaps that should not even be our prayer. Perhaps their beauty would overwhelm us too much. Instead, maybe our prayer should be for stolen moments that allow us to glimpse and briefly comprehend their glory and for time to savor our memories of those moments.

My friend Alan Haras, a spiritual director and yoga teacher, defines *beauty* as that which draws us out of ourselves and into the Divine Mystery, where we discover ourselves anew in the mystery of God. In an interview with Krista Tippett, John O'Donohue describes beauty as "that in the presence of which we feel more alive."[2] O'Donohue asserts that what our culture tends to think of as beauty, like the air-brushed body on the cover of a magazine, is really glamour.

My baby shrieking in delight, her face smeared with butternut squash, is not glamorous; but, oh, is she beautiful! My five-year-old with crooked teeth, sleep in his eyes, hair sticking up, and a radiant smile is not glamorous; but, oh, is he beautiful! My three-year-old's impish grin, wrinkly pink knees from the cuts and abrasions that knit themselves back together, and silvery scars from long-ago falls do not make him glamorous; but, oh, is he beautiful! My pulse quickens at the sight of each of my children. Life leaps within me in recognition. Holy calls out to holy, deep to deep. They aren't just beautiful; they *are* beauty.

Tell Your Story

Reflect on the beauty of your children. How do they stir your heart with their magnificence? When does their beauty feel like too much to bear?

The Marks We Bear

When Jesus was resurrected from the dead, he bore the wounds of the crucifixion: holes in his hands and feet and a gaping wound in his side. Thomas put his fingers in that pain-filled place and knew it was his Teacher. Our wounds, our scars, and our marks hold a place in how we are known. They tell our story. They hold our history.

As a mother, I bear marks too. My hips are wider, my stomach softer, my breasts less full. My body has been stretched and pulled. After birthing three children, it is comfortable in this saggier place and hasn't "bounced back" to its prior form. I used to have naturally curly hair that I loved. After Declan was born, the curls went away for more than six years. When I would try to style my newly, oddly straight hair, I longed for the ease of the days when I could just let the curls air dry.

As much as they have changed my body, my kids have yet to cause me physical scars—although every time my fifteen-month-old makes a move to bite me, that could change. They've changed me without, and they've marked me within. They have taught me of my frailty and my weaknesses. I have learned from them the edges of my humanity: how much I need sleep and quiet, how little I'm really capable of.

I bear the grief of their falls, their illnesses, and their ER visits. I bear the wounds of their anxieties, their fears, their angers, and their hurts. I bear the marks of one who desperately wants to protect them, to keep them safe and pain-free; but who must open them to the world, companion them, and walk alongside and even behind them, holding back my desire to rush ahead and smooth their path. These marks convey who I am now. I am grateful for how they tell my story.

Tell Your Story

How have your children marked you? What scars do you bear within and without? How do those markings tell your story as a mother?

Liminal Space

When we become mothers, we cross one of life's major thresholds. And we stay there, right on that threshold, every single day. We enter what's called *liminal space*, the in-between.

To be in a liminal space is to remain on the edge, to never enter a comfortable middle ground. Our children are always changing, and the boundary of parenthood is always moving. We are in constant transition, and we never reach certainty. It seems we never leave liminal space. Every time we hit a groove in our parenting, every time we think we've figured out one thing, something else changes. My children are still relatively small, but my friends whose children are teenagers have assured me it never gets easier. It just becomes different.

I find it exhausting to live in this in-between place where I can never simply rest in how things are. Sometimes I feel resentful. I wish for some stability and that my kids would stop growing and changing just for a little bit until I can catch my breath.

And then I hear the whispered invitation to rest in God and let God be my source of consistency. God reminds me that liminality frees me from the notion that I can be in control. Liminal space wrests control away from my ego, the part of me that wants to hold the reins, figure things out, and keep myself at the center of it all. Even as the change and growth in my life bewilders me, it frees me to encounter my true self, to meet the Holy Spirit in me, and to meet God in my kids. I find grace in recognizing that I cannot be at the center and in recognizing the divine flame whose eternal presence is the only constant.

Tell Your Story

How is parenting a liminal space for you? What changes do you see your children living out in this season? What centers and grounds you as you live in the in-between?

In the Slipstream

Ronan and Healy's births and early months of life were far easier for me than Declan's. Their births brought a threshold holiness too, but I didn't feel so completely lost and my children weren't as unknown or bewildering to me. Patterns of behavior had been worn into my brain and my body. I could draw on muscle memory that told my body how to push at the end of labor and how to nurse, and my body more readily produced milk. As I paced the floor with them at night, I held the real, lived knowledge that this was just a season that would pass, no matter how all-encompassing it felt.

Despite its liminality, motherhood is highly repetitive. Again and again I make meals, sing songs, read stories, pack bags, buckle car seats, and weather temper tantrums. An ease results from all this practice, and in some moments I find myself gliding through the paces like I'm in a slipstream of current, not fighting or pushing. I know how to move through our bedtime routine. I have *Mercy Watson:*

Princess in Disguise memorized, and I can do the voices of the characters in my sleep.

The liminal nature of parenting can feel like waves. Sometimes they toss me around, but sometimes I can ride them. I can glide along with them, following their curves to the shore. I now know I am one who can ride the waves. I am one who can weather the boredom and the frustration, the laughter and the tears. I can handle both the repetitive days and the mercurial nature of my children.

In my first years of motherhood, when someone called me "Mom" I would want to look behind me to see if he or she were talking to someone else. I didn't recognize myself in that title. Now, with all this practice, I am no longer surprised when people refer to me as a mom or a mother. I am living into my motherhood.

Tell Your Story

In what ways have you found your groove as a mother? When do you find yourself in the slipstream of parenting? What is that like for you?

Breathe into Trust

Some days, when I try to check in with how I really am, I can't see beyond survival mode. I barely can catch my breath before the next day hits. I can go for a long time without feeling the divine spark in my relationship with my children.

I may be fully present in each moment—present to the joy of Healy's laugh, the sweetness of Declan and Ronan's play, the frustration of the mess of our house, and the pain in my back as I walk around the room yet again, holding Healy's hand as she learns to walk—but I am also thinking ahead: *When will I unload the dishwasher? What should I next feed them? When will Nick be home? What meetings are coming up?* I try to balance our schedule and their needs, both immediate and long-term, with the experience of this exact moment: in the winter that they are five, three, and one, when it is six degrees outside and they are full of pent-up energy.

In these overwhelming and exhausting moments, being present to Jesus, being awake to the deep in me that cries out to the deep in them, and listening to the movement of the Holy Spirit all feel like just more things to do when I have no capacity for even one more thing. It is as if I am keeping eight plates spinning in the air—just barely—and if I try to work in a ninth plate, they'll all come crashing down.

Since I can't add another focus when these moments overwhelm me, I try to breathe into a sense of trust and believe that the holy is unfolding in me anyway, regardless of whether I am aware of it. I trust that by living this life of motherhood's sacrificial love, I am drawing closer to God and becoming more like Jesus.

Tell Your Story

When you are in hard seasons, what helps you trust that this work is holy? How do you connect to a sense of God-with-you amid the chaos of daily life?

Be with What Is

A bird feeder hangs on our front porch outside the living room window. It is a large and quite popular bird feeder. I often notice ten black-capped chickadees and sparrows perched on it at a time, with thirty or forty more waiting in the tree branches.

I love glancing up from playing with the kids to see the riot of feathers through the window. They connect me with nature and God's creation, if only for a moment. I enjoy the ritual of filling the feeder: lifting it carefully from its perch, opening the stainless-steel bin of bird feed, filling the scoop, feeling the silky dust of corn and seed on my fingers, and listening to the gentle whir of the seed as it fills the container. My heart rate slows, my breathing deepens, and I feel connected to the Creator as I care for a little bit of creation. I can experience the presence of God so easily and so fully in such gentle and mundane tasks—unless my children are outside. Then it's the chaos of

"Can I help you?"

"My brother took my scoop!"

"Oops, I spilled it!"

"No, it's *my* turn now!"

"Can I eat some birdseed?"

"Can I play in it?"

"When will you be done?"

In these moments, the ways I've been taught to connect to the holy, to slow down and be present, fail me. Yet surely this moment is charged with God's presence as my children bring the Holy Spirit that dwells in them to the task.

I feel challenged, then, to be present to what *is,* to celebrate and live into *this* holy reality that includes mediating fights, keeping hands out of bird poop, and stopping birdseed from spilling everywhere. When I recognize my more chaotic moments as opportunities to flow within this reality, I can experience the presence of the Holy Spirit.

Tell Your Story

What is life like in your home? What messes and chaos and joys and frustrations mark your day-to-day life? How might you respond to the invitation to be with what is and see it all as holy?

Become Like Water

One morning, Ronan decided he would make me mad. He was frustrated with me—too many requests met with *no*s—and I watched him choose to wind me up.

He started by raising his voice louder and louder, trying to elicit a reaction. Then he began to throw things. When I told him to stop, he yelled, "No!" and watched for my response.

Often when he wants to wind me up, he is successful. I yell right back. This morning, though, I imagined a clear lake of life-giving water. Imagining water reminds me of my desire to be like water for my children. I want to be a flowing river that brings life to my children's growing bodies and changeable natures. I picture within me a clear, deep pool that can offer them and myself calm, stillness, and respite when they rage.

When I successfully held inside me that image, I could draw on my soul's depth and stillness and refreshment, and I responded calmly to Ronan's outburst. We went through our usual discipline routine, so in some ways this moment was no different than any other. But it felt like a gift to him, to myself, and to my other children (who were witnessing our altercation) to interact with him from an internal place of peace. I showed him shelter, a safe place to storm, and how to experience consequences while still being loved. My children saw that I can meet their hurt and their anger with peace and love and acceptance.

This is not how these moments always or even usually go; when they do go well, I want to celebrate the grace of the peaceful moment and the gift that the vision of peaceful water can be to me and to my children. Today, my prayer is this: *May I be a river, free of attachments, flowing lavishly and abundantly through the day, moving with your currents, and bringing life and refreshment to my children. Amen.*

Tell Your Story

How have you been like water for your children? In what ways have you provided refreshment for them? How could you celebrate the ways you find peace and calm as you flow through your days?

Shimmering Moments

Recently I was cleaning in the kitchen, and Healy came in and tugged on my shirt. She seemed to want a snack. She pointed and babbled, so I handed her a bag of coconut chips and continued to wash the dishes.

Then she pulled on my shirt again. When I squatted down to talk to her, she pushed me to the floor and climbed onto my lap.

Healy is an active, independent child, and this may be the first time she has willfully climbed into my arms. So I sat with her. We shared the coconut chips, passing the bag back and forth. I rubbed her back and savored the weight and the warmth of her on my lap and the way I could feel her heart beating. Though I noticed the dirty kitchen floor, I chose to let it go. The Spirit in her called out to the Spirit within me, and I savored the sweetness.

On another afternoon, as Healy sat at the bottom of the steps, I started to sing a simple song about the sounds the heart makes. She stopped playing, looked at me with the biggest smile, and leaned her head into mine so our foreheads touched. My hair fell around us, creating a dark, sacred space of deep connection, and we nuzzled into each other.

I kept singing, and she pulsed in and out, pulling back to make eye contact and smile, then leaning in to touch and cuddle. It was a gift of pure grace for both of us. It lasted perhaps five minutes, but those five minutes were charged with the presence of the Holy Spirit.

In these moments, I remember that mothering is not something I do *to* the kids; it is something I participate in *with* them. Our relationship flows as a holy and mysterious endeavor crafted between us, and we create something new. When these shimmering moments happen, I don't want to miss them. I want to be awake to the gift of their reminder that the parent-child relationship is holy.

Tell Your Story

When have you experienced moments of deep connection with your children? What is it like to let yourself sink into the holiness of these moments as they unfold?

Sitting with Mary

I have a statue of Mary that makes my soul sing. This white stone statue on a dark wooden base depicts Mary on her knees tenderly curled around her infant son. Cradled in her arms, Jesus is alert and engaged and tugs on her hair. Their intimacy is breathtaking. I yearn for my intimate moments with my children to radiate such intense holy love. And I long for that closeness with Jesus.

Mary can be an uncomfortable figure to approach in prayer, laden as she is with the baggage of various spiritual traditions; differing viewpoints cloud our vision of her. But when I set aside what I think I know of her and simply approach her, mother to mother, I find she has much to teach me. Better than anyone, Mary knows what it is to mother and care for God's beloved child.

Mary's curled and protective posture speaks to me of the domestic nature of mothering. She radiates a peace that says she is right where she is meant to be. While I do not want my children to be my whole world, sometimes they are. On those all-encompassing days, I long to know what Mary seems to know—being there for them is enough. In my statue, Mary is lost in the moment with her son, and she inspires me to lose myself with my children, to abandon myself to their joyful and demanding presence.

As I gaze at that baby boy tugging on Mary's hair, I envy Mary's intimacy with Jesus—her nearness to him and how she knew him so well in every moment of his young life. I don't wish to have been Jesus' mother, but I do long for such stunning love and closeness with Jesus. I desire to know his heart as Mary does. I strive to love my children in the same way.

Tell Your Story

As you contemplate Mary and her mothering of Jesus, what arises in you? What might Mary reveal to you of your own mothering?

PART II
Becoming Yourself

Awakening to Self

When I am pregnant, I can feel my soul hibernating. It is as if the deepest part of me crawls into a cave and sleeps. It feels like a death. I am reminded of Revelation 12:14: "The woman was given the two wings of a great eagle, so that she might fly to the place prepared for her in the wilderness, where she would be taken care of for a time, times and half a time, out of the serpent's reach" (NIV). Like the woman in the desert, pregnancy is for me a time of hiding in the wilderness, a time outside of time. It is the only time my mind is naturally quiet, my thoughts stilled. Instead of the usual chatter, I only hear white noise: *shhh*.

The first time I was pregnant, I found this disquieting and eerie, and I didn't recognize myself. If my thoughts were gone, what remained? Now, after five pregnancies—two miscarriages and three full-term—I've learned to name the internal silence for the hibernation it is, and I know how to wade my way through it and survive.

After birth and the first few sleepless months, I begin to awaken to myself. I start to create new ideas, feel emotions beyond fatigue, and experience desires beyond sleep. Finally, after this third birth, I can name this experience as my own becoming, a birthing back into myself. I've learned not to race ahead and not to judge myself as my thoughts come back and I reawaken, the same yet different.

Tell Your Story

Remember your moments of awakening. When have you begun to feel yourself coming awake again after becoming a mother?

Coming Home to Yourself

A friend of mine is the mother of a two-and-a-half-year-old and a five-month-old. When we ran into each other at the library and discussed our lives, she said, "This weekend was *good*. It was the first time I felt like myself, instead of just a mom—not that I don't love being a mom!" Five months after her younger daughter joined their family, she began to awaken to herself, to experience her own birth. Another friend, whose youngest is five years old, recently described her related desire to figure out her identity apart from being the mother of her three children.

Whether your time of awakening happens months or years after giving birth, you will likely experience a sense of being born back into the fullness of your self-identity. I think of it as a homecoming, a returning to who you are.

Your awakening may take different forms. You may experience it as frustration and restlessness or as an awareness of your soul coming back online after months of sleep deprivation. You may feel curious about your identity. You may be able to enjoy again a food that had become repulsive in pregnancy or find yourself delighting in something you have always loved but hadn't been able to enjoy in the swirl of early parenthood. The first time I pick up a novel after giving birth and disappear into a fictional world, I meet myself again. *There you are,* I think. *Welcome back.*

You are coming back home to yourself. You have poured out yourself in care for your children. In those early months and years, you've been consumed by their holy fire. You have forgotten yourself and died to yourself. You have been broken apart and are now being reconstituted. Can you hear the invitation to new life? However this beginning looks and feels for you, know that it is just that: a beginning. Our becoming is ongoing. We continue to be created and formed.

Tell Your Story

What are the ways you've begun to feel like yourself again? How is your new self emerging? What is it like to come back home to yourself? How is your awakening self-identity an echo of the person you've always been?

You Are a
Divine Spark

Throughout one magical spring break, I took my children on daily outings that included horseback riding and a trip to the Columbus Zoo. The zoo has a charming, historic wooden carousel, and my children begged to ride it. After they all spun around on their chosen creatures to the calliope music, Ronan was overcome with excitement.

"That was awesome!" he shouted, bounding with delight. "It was even better than riding a real horse! The only thing more awesome than the carousel is God!"

He lit up with the divine flame; the Holy Spirit leaped within him. His body even moved like a flame, jumping and twisting in joy.

I can recognize the divine flame easily in my children; they so transparently bear the image of God as they display holiness from within and without. It is harder for me to remember that I too carry the divine flame. I may not leap with my body, but my heart leaps with joy when I encounter the presence of the Lord. As I celebrate the spark in my children, I am learning to celebrate and nurture it within me.

You carry the divine spark too. Only you can tend to and care for the holiness within you. Part of learning to notice and nurture your divine flame includes noticing your warning signs, the small signals that let you know you need a break from your children and space to recenter in your identity in Christ. Snapping at my kids quickly or easily indicates that my fuse is short. My sense of oxygen and space is another warning sign. I ask myself, *Do I feel like I have enough air to breathe?*

Your children can always take more than you can give and will always need more than you have, so know when to wave the white flag and ask for help. Each person's "tells" are unique. Ask for time for yourself *before* you are at the end of your rope. Only we know what diminishes the divine spark we carry within us.

Tell Your Story

How do your body and mind let you know that you need a break? What are your simple, life-giving, practices that tend your divine spark? How have these practices changed since becoming a mother?

The Need for Space

I can measure my well-being by how high the ceiling feels and whether there seems to be enough air in the room to breathe comfortably. On days when I am alone with my children, the ceiling starts to drop at about 4:00 p.m., and it seems to get lower and squeeze air out of the room as we all become more irritable. I understand why so many parents call the hour before dinner "the witching hour;" no one is content.

I notice this shortness of breath and tempers and the feeling of low ceilings other times too: when I haven't slept well the night before; when a child is in a bad mood and cannot snap out of it; on Thursdays; when plans fall through.

Parenting is a delicate dance of meeting the physical and emotional needs of each person while also keeping the house in order, nurturing growth, investing in relationship, and sometimes just surviving. When this complex, well-oiled machine does not run quite as it should and the ceiling seems to drop and push air out of the room, I long for spaciousness. I dream of light and fresh air and a sense of freedom, of space and time to pull in deep breaths. On those days, I have learned to find "quiet time" by myself after Nick gets home. I'll go for a run or a walk, take a bath, or sit with a candle for ten minutes of silence while I breathe slowly and deeply.

I find spaciousness within experiences that remind me that I am cared for and not alone, and when I can see that what I give my children is meaningful. Open space helps me to come home to myself. And then I can experience the reality of being held by God—God's loving presence becomes an embodied knowing instead of just words. When I can hold onto that sense of God with me and me with God, I experience a spaciousness that feels like a fresh breeze dancing through the windows.

Tell Your Story

How do you foster spaciousness in your days? What helps you feel like there is enough oxygen in the room? How do you recognize God's working through your feelings of space and breath?

The Need for Others

Iarrived at the opening retreat for my spiritual direction training program excited, nervous, and anxious to find my place in this new community. We opened our time together with a circle of welcome. As I looked at the faces of these strangers who would be my teachers and classmates for the next two years, I wondered about the relationships I would form before focusing my gaze on the altar at our center.

On the table was a statue of Mary and Elizabeth roughly carved out of stone. The two pregnant cousins bend toward each other and embrace in greeting; their faces light up with joy. In their welcoming each other, I felt Mary and Elizabeth welcome me into a space of soul learning, and I knew I was right where I was supposed to be. My nerves and anxiety quieted. I belonged in that circle.

Through my training and practice, Mary and Elizabeth's relationship has become for me a symbol of spiritual direction, of the way the holy in me rises to meet the holy in another. I picture Jesus and John kicking in joyful recognition from within the waters of their mothers' wombs, and I experience that same "kick" of recognition and awe as I hear directees' stories and enter the sacred ground of their lives.

These two cousins have whispered to me of the importance of keeping companions on the journey. They remind me of the strength I have found in traveling with fellow mothers. I imagine the fatigue and loneliness of Mary and Elizabeth's pregnancies in the months before they reconnected. Then I recognize the reassurance of having a soul friend who can say, "Me too! You are not alone." Our journeys are richer and more joyful for being shared.

Tell Your Story

With whom have you shared the road of motherhood? How have your mothering companions lightened and enriched your life as a mother?

Who Are You Today?

I am deeply curious about who my kids will become. I delight when I glimpse new aspects of their personalities: the things that bring them joy or pain, the ways they interact with one another, and the ways they interact with God. Each time I catch a new glimpse of their character, I marvel at it and savor the moment of discovery as much as I can within the chaotic dance of family life. I wonder, *Is this who you are?* I try to hold my curiosity lightly alongside patience, a peace in the not-yet-knowing, and a delight in the mystery.

I would like to hold my own soul in that same gentle way and allow it to become who it is meant to be as I hold it with open, loving hands. I'd like to wonder at and honor the mystery of my own becoming just as I strive to do for my children. When I remember to bring curiosity to my own identity, I ask myself: *Who am I today? And today? And today?*

Today I am the mother of Declan, Ronan, and Healy. I am Nick's wife. I am a spiritual director. I am a writer. I'm a listener, a lover, an empathizer, and a connection-maker. I am curious, open, and loving. I used to think I was smart, but today I'm afraid my kids have made me dumb. I love story, mystery, God, nature, and my family. I am a woman whose heart is full.

Today I am learning to be gentler with myself, to not hold myself to higher standards than I do everyone else, to know the things I need in place to maintain emotional and mental health, and to accept my humanity and my weaknesses and honor them by eating, sleeping, and moving my body.

I am trying. I do my best every day and hope it will be enough.

This is who I am today. This is how far I can see of who I am becoming.

Tell Your Story

Take time to wonder: Who are you today? Ponder or write or speak of where you find your identity this day. What can you name of who you are?

The Mystery of Becoming

I have a painting of Saint Brendan's boat in my writing nook. Legend has it that Saint Brendan, an early Irish monastic, built a boat and set out to find Eden. On his journey, he had no map and did not navigate. He simply went where the wind took him and trusted God to lead him through the breeze. In the painting, the boat's sails glow gold, as if lit from within by the fire of the Holy Spirit.

For years, these golden sails have helped me to quiet my heart, enter into prayer, and wait for the winds of the Holy Spirit to lead me. I imagine the ocean into which the boat sails as a representation of the heart and soul of the great I AM—as vast as the sea. As I follow the Spirit's guidance further into the sea, I get to know more of God each day; but there will always be more to learn and to explore.

Attending to the mystery of becoming is like pushing our boats a little bit further into the sea of knowing God each day. Our souls are likewise vast and full of the mystery and wisdom that God has given us. We are always learning more and becoming more of who we are. We find that our identity as mother and woman and image-bearer of the divine is slowly and continually brought into the light.

When I imagine my journey with God and with my children as a boat sailing on the ocean, the winds of the Holy Spirit guiding it where it will, I feel freer. I can give myself more grace in my parenting and not be so hard on myself when I mess up. I release the expectation that I have all the answers or know the "right" way to do things. When regret begins to rise in me over a harsh word or a sharp tone I've used with my children, I remind myself to honor those hard moments as part of the becoming. God calls me into being—continues to create me—through them. I can let go of control, of trying to figure out who I am or what I am meant to do, and trust that in time God will reveal to me the fullness of who I'm being created to be.

Tell Your Story

Where do you feel the winds of the Holy Spirit leading you? How do these leadings guide you to new and surprising aspects of your identity and your life?

Yourself Apart
from Them

As a mother, I often split my attention between multiple things at once: the two or three children speaking to me, the meal that needs to be prepared, the house that needs to be cleaned, and the bag that needs to be packed for that day's adventures. Although I have become comfortable with these continuous demands for my attention, they help me receive my work in spiritual direction, where I sit with my undivided attention on one other person, as a gift. My spiritual direction room is a place to be still, to listen deeply, and to focus on my experience of God's presence. I am glad to leave my children behind for that window of time.

We are full human beings. We are complete in ourselves and complete before God without our children. We can find it uncomfortable to name this reality when so much of our identity, and who the world sees us as being, comes from our children and in our mothering.

When Declan was four weeks old, a friend came over to watch him so I could go for a slow run—my first time exercising since giving birth. It was a beautiful day, and I savored the blue sky and the cool breeze on my sweating skin. I marveled at how easily and lightly I moved with no baby in my belly, in my arms, or in a stroller. Maneuvering just one body from place to place felt like flying. But after less than a mile, I felt the invisible tether that dances between me and Declan pull uncomfortably tight. I couldn't bear to move one step farther from him.

The ties between us and our children are strong; yet we are independent beings, seen and loved by God for ourselves. To be present to our children, to recognize their identities as they are now and as God is creating them to be, we must be fully present to ourselves as well. Letting out the line between us and our children gives us space to be on our own, remember who we were before children, and experience who we are now. Time away from our children moves us out of the swirling winds of parenthood into shelter that allows space for each of our individual identities to flourish.

Tell Your Story

Who are you apart from your children? What parts of your life do you not share with them? How does experiencing your separateness create space to enjoy the time spent together?

The Whisper of Desire

Paying attention to what we want can be a subversive act. As women and as Christians, we might learn that desires are "bad," that they can mislead us, and that they are meant to be controlled, subdued, and ignored. But Saint Ignatius encouraged his followers to listen to and pray for their desires. He realized that God can communicate with us in any form, including our emotions.

Noticing what we want, then, is a radical spiritual practice. Not all our desires are God-given, but we can discern the difference by praying about our desires, asking for what we want, and recognizing how our desires shift over time.

Listening to our heart's desires can be as challenging and awkward as exercising again after childbirth. We may be out of practice and out of touch with ourselves. You may find it easiest to begin by naming your physical desires, noticing what your body wants. As you practice listening to your body, you will become more attuned to your deeper desires.

For the first year after each of my children were born, I only wanted one thing: sleep. Every time I tried to name my desires, I could not get past that one deeply-longed-for word. I would try to visualize what I wanted and pictured myself curled in bed, sleeping peacefully without interruption. Only now, when my youngest is nearly two, do I have a sense of other desires: connection with others, deep relationships, time in nature, silence and solitude, a frequent good cup of coffee. As I notice and honor these longings, I can begin to hear the desire that rests beneath them: my heart crying out for Jesus' companionship. I can only hear my deepest longing for a connection between my heart and the heart of God when I have allowed my other desires to surface first. When I can name my desires, I can see the source of the need they seek to meet: time to be close to God.

Tell Your Story

Give yourself permission to ask these questions: What do I long for? Who do I desire to be? What do I yearn to find time and space for? When you can name these, wonder about how they might point to even deeper desires.

When Desires Change

For many years, I dreamed of having the courage to write. For me, the pinnacle of those dreams, the Holy Grail of writing, was a novel: a story that would bring the richness and holiness of the mundane to life and would move people the way my favorite novels have moved me.

I finally began working toward this dream a few years before I had kids. After years of writing in my journal, "I want to write, but I don't know what to write," I caught the tail of a story: an image of two sisters, their differences, and their deep love for each other. I worked as a freelance consultant at the time; during the weeks I didn't have work, I would pour myself into the story of these sisters as they grew from children to adults. I imagined their world, and it became a place as real to me as my own life; the coffee shop in which I wrote faded away as I created their small Ohio town.

Several months after Declan was born, I picked up my novel again. Working on it had brought me a sense of fullness and freedom, and I couldn't wait to get back to it. I thought it would be a way of coming home to myself. But try as I might to reenter that fictional universe, I couldn't find my way in. The world that had once been so real had become false and hollow.

At first I was sad and frustrated. I thought I wasn't trying hard enough. I was afraid the writing part of my identity had died. But once I faced my initial disappointment, I saw that my heart had shifted. I no longer dreamed of writing a novel. What was once my Holy Grail is now just a tin cup. I realized that I still longed to write, but I no longer wanted to bring to life any moment other than those with my children—their playing in the backyard and coloring with chalk and making one another laugh.

It has been surprising and humbling to see a dream I nurtured since childhood become dust and drift away. I was just as surprised and humbled at its resurrection. I began confessing to my journal once again, "I want to write, but I don't know what to write," until I finally recognized God's invitation to write *this* book. I am and I am not the person I was before becoming a mother.

Tell Your Story

How have your desires changed since becoming a mother? How have these changes surprised you?

Becoming Real

As a child, I understood *The Velveteen Rabbit* to be a story about growing up and the power of love. I equated the rabbit's "realness" with maturity, which I saw grow through the child's love as if the rabbit were growing up alongside the boy who loved him.

I still see those themes in the story, but now I also read it as a profound symbol of motherhood. In loving our children, we become ragged, inside and out. We pay much less attention to our physical form because we give so much attention to the physical forms of our children. Our bodies age and sag. We wear and tear on the inside, our nerves fray, our hearts stretch and break, and our capacity for love and joy and anger and sorrow increases exponentially.

In our wearing down and wearing out, we become more real; we bear less pretense and more heart. In the hiddenness of my home, where I rock my children back to sleep at one o'clock in the morning, and again at three and five, there is no room for a false version of myself. My children are without pretense, and they have stripped me of my own.

When I met people before I had children, a voice in my head asked, *What do they think of me? What are they seeing when they look at me? Do they like me?* That low-level worry clouded my ability to be present. Now when I meet another person, I am curious about how they are doing. The once-dominant voice of concern about how others perceive me is now barely a whisper. I can focus on what others say to me. I notice their joy or pain, and I notice what response their emotions stir up within me. By moving deeper into myself, I've quieted my worrying, self-doubtful voice. My self-consciousness and insecurities are no longer in charge of my interactions with others.

I am still as human as I was before children, and I'm grouchy as often as I am content. But I feel much freer from expectation and from false senses of identity. It feels holy. Like the Velveteen Rabbit, I see the ways my caring for those I love has made me more real.

Tell Your Story

How has becoming a mother made you more real? How have you become less false or less hidden behind pretense? What is it like for you to meet your real self?

Delight in Who You Are

I did not find my true identity until after I had my first child. Before becoming a mom, I focused on working, performing, and being who I thought I should be. But in the desert of the "fourth trimester," I met myself. When everything I'd once busied myself with was stripped away—my work, my social life, my rest—I easily jettisoned my superficial traits and habits and named the pieces of my identity that I missed during pregnancy and needed in my life to feel whole.

I missed talking with people. I missed time to connect with the mystery of God. I missed the sense of purpose I felt when companioning someone through a hard time. I missed story. In recognizing what felt missing, I realized how they connect to my deepest gifts—gifts of listening, presence, mystery, and wonder. My recognition of these gifts became an invitation to a new, life-giving career as a spiritual director. Spiritual direction feels more "me" than anything I had done before. I have found what I am meant to do.

And yet, for perhaps the first time, I also knew that my work would never be all of me. As I fed my son in the middle of the night, I breathed deeply and marveled at the experience of holding him and being held by God. I finally understood that I did not need to accomplish or prove anything because in my weakness and my strength, I am enough—enough for myself, enough for my son, enough for God.

In naming our gifts and experiencing ourselves as enough, we honor God's work of creation. My spiritual director often asks me: "Have you allowed God to thank you?" Her question can remind us to create space to hear God's gratitude for the ways we choose to share life with God. It can be difficult to let God thank us for the work we do, to let God enjoy who we've been created to be, and to enjoy for ourselves who God has made us to be. Yet listening for and experiencing God's love and gratitude helps us see ourselves more clearly. When I see myself through God's loving eyes, I am filled with joy and awe: I like who I see.

Tell Your Story

How has having children changed you and introduced you to your true self? How can you delight in who God created you to be? What might God want to thank you for?

PART III
Becoming Holy

The Holy Tension

Our spiritual journeys often consist of deep paradox: great joy and great sorrow, new invitations alongside loss and grief, feeling at home and feeling like an outsider—the list goes on and on. My work in spiritual direction has shown me that God meets us in the space between these uncomfortable tensions.

I've fallen in love with the both/and of holding together life's paradoxes. The Holy Spirit often moves in this tension of the in-between, of the third way, of the space between certainties. Embracing the both/and reminds us that we are not in control. Paradoxes invite us to let go and create space for surprise.

Our rational, thinking brains are uncomfortable with these paradoxes. We like resolution, but we often cannot resolve holy tensions. We can only hold them. When we do, we begin to engage the world from our souls, where we encounter relationship with God. Paradox takes us out of head knowledge and into heart knowledge.

We continually find the both/and in our parenting. Motherhood lives in holy tension, where our greatest strengths meet our greatest weakness and where we are most human and broken and most divine. We lose our sense of self to find ourselves. We experience the greatest love and the greatest heartbreak. We experience great awe and profound boredom—often within minutes of each other! Motherhood's constant paradox creates a deep potential for holiness.

When I think I have the answers, it is much harder for me to experience God's presence. I'm not looking for God because I already have it figured out, or I at least think I do. But when there is no right answer, I am forced back into curiosity. Tension and paradox invite us into wonder and humility, which help us to be more receptive to God's presence.

Thankfully, I rarely think I have it figured out as a mother. My children are walking paradoxes, both the most angelic and the most challenging beings I have ever encountered. In this life of holy tension, in my confusion and discomfort, when I wish there was an easy either/or, God speaks to me through the both/and.

Tell Your Story

How are you experiencing both/and in your mothering today? What holy tensions are you holding? What is it like to bear these paradoxes?

Strong and Weak

At a recent blessing for a woman preparing to birth her first child, my friend Megan shared about the way becoming a mother has changed her relationship with her body.

"I feel so much stronger now," she said, "so much more impressed by my own body. I don't judge it anymore, because it's amazing! I feel capable of anything!"

She gave words to what so many of us who have children have experienced: We are *strong*. We can finally let go of having the "perfect" body—because who cares! None of the aesthetics compare to what our bodies have shown us we're capable of doing. Our boundaries have exploded. Our sense of our limits has been pushed beyond measure. Childbirth is just one way to experience our maternal strength. We are homes for our children, our muscles toned by our constant lifting and holding, our backs and arms and legs strengthened through our love. We are invited into a holy awe toward ourselves.

Then we encounter our weakness: Our deep, human need for sleep. The edges of our emotional well-being when we don't get enough rest. The weakness of our temper and the guilt or shame we feel when we yell at our children for small and ridiculous offenses, which make us feel small and ridiculous too.

Parenting is amplifying. It expands our strengths, and it expands our weaknesses. I feel so much more capable, stronger, and wiser than I ever have before—and I feel so much weaker and dumber, more limited and flawed. I've never been so intimate and comfortable with both my virtues and my flaws. God is present in that tension. Our weaknesses invite us to lean into God, to know that we cannot and need not do it alone. Weaknesses remind us of our human limits and our dependence. But God comes in our strength too. Like all our virtues, our strength is a grace from the Lord, a gift of the Holy Spirit, who lives in us. May we see our moments of strength and our moments of weakness as invitations to draw more closely to God.

Tell Your Story

Consider the ways you've encountered your physical limits as a mother. When have you come face to face with your weaknesses? When have you been surprised by your strength?

Mary and Martha

Growing up, I found the story of Jesus' visit to Mary and Martha's home challenging and frustrating. Martha works hard to make things just right for their visitors, and she becomes increasingly annoyed with her sister who sits and listens to Jesus. When Martha turns to Jesus for help, he chides her and tells her that Mary has "chosen the better part." (See Luke 10:38-42.)

I was a perfectionist and an overachiever, a typical oldest child, and I just knew that if Jesus came to visit, I would want to make sure everything was perfect for him. I felt like Jesus' response to Martha wasn't particularly compassionate or helpful. After all, if it weren't for Martha, what would he eat?

As a young adult, I recognized the gift of presence and a calling to be with people, to sit and listen deeply. I realized I was more like Mary than I had ever known. Suddenly, Mary didn't seem so lazy! Maybe Martha *is* working too hard. Maybe she needs to relax.

Today, as a mom to three young children, I see the pitting of the two sisters against each other as an unhelpful paradigm. Instead of the either/or, I wonder about the both/and. I feel like both Mary and Martha as I encounter Christ in my children. From moment to moment I vary between channeling more of Mary's spirit or of Martha's spirit in my parenting. Sometimes I am content to sit with my children and savor their presence. Other times, if I don't get up and get moving, I know we won't have any food to eat for dinner or clean clothes to wear.

I am not Mary, and I am not Martha. I am both, flowing through the day, trying to live into wherever God is inviting me to be: to sit with God's presence within my children, to be present to the Holy Spirit stirring within me, and to do my work when it is time to work.

Tell Your Story

When are you Martha? When are you Mary? How do you feel them both living within you? When do they share space peacefully, and when do they battle for attention?

Time That Crawls and Time That Flies

Children change our sense of time. "The days are long but the years are short." I interrupted the first person who rehearsed this classic parenting saying to me.

"The days are long," they began.

"But the nights are longer?" I replied.

The days, the hours, and the minutes can drag. I often feel exhausted, like I'm sick of the kids and they're sick of me, and no one has any patience left. Then I glance at the clock and realize it's not even 8:30 a.m. I think, *There is no way it is still morning.*

In other moments, I realize how much time with my children has passed that I've barely noticed. When Ronan turned four, we watched the video of two-year-old Declan meeting him for the first time. I could not believe four years of life had slipped by. We all experience time's inconsistencies, and children somehow heighten the phenomenon.

They amplify time's quickness and drag down its slowest, second-by-second passing.

I recognize God's working in time's strange ability to slow down and speed up. I see in my children glimmers of the One who is outside of time. Surreal moments of warped time with my children remind me to connect with God.

Sometimes I connect with God by being fully present to the moment, dwelling inside of time: I notice what happens in each moment as I watch golden sunlight stream through the window, breathe deeply as I prepare breakfast, listen to my children's stories, and mediate their fights.

Other times I connect with God by getting lost in time. I lose track of the minutes when I get lost in the book I read out loud to the boys as they cuddle up on either side of me, or when I watch the children dash in and out of the waves and dig in the sand at the beach, or when we explore the woods together.

My children help me experience God's presence inside and outside of time. They pull me out of my thoughts and into the present moment, and their sweet creativity invites me to slip outside of time with them to get lost in play, imagination, story, and prayer.

Tell Your Story

How has parenting bent your perception of time? How could these moments with your children be an invitation to prayer?

Scarcity and Abundance

In a recent conversation, a good friend mentioned that her counselor asked her whether she was operating out of scarcity or abundance. *Yes*, I thought to myself. *Both.*

I find myself vacillating between scarcity and abundance over the course of the days and weeks. I operate out of abundance when I get enough sleep, when the kids are healthy, and when I can find time to pray and write. But abundance feels more delicate and tenuous than I would like, and I can easily slip into scarcity mode.

Over Memorial Day weekend I experienced that quick swing from one to the next. The weekend began with abundance—time together as a family and time to myself, time to exercise and time to rest and play—but swerved to scarcity when Healy, just four months old, fell off the couch. The sound of her head hitting the wood floor was awful, and she cried so hard, for so long.

My heart ached for her, and I was scared she might be badly injured. She was fine—*thank you, Lord, she was fine*—but it wasn't how I thought I'd spend my afternoon: scared and sad and trying to keep my baby calm at the hospital as I explained to one person after another what had happened.

After we returned home, I sat in silence and tried to invite God into the experience. I prayed for an open heart and felt how much pain was there, how heavy my heart was, and how hard it was to open it. I wept. I knew my fear and sadness weren't needed anymore—they'd served their purpose—but they still needed to work their way through my heart and blood and muscles and bones. My sense of abundance shriveled up and dried out. I was a husk, not a fruit.

I am learning just how fluid my senses of scarcity and abundance really are, and I am trying not to grasp at either. I am finding a spiritual practice in breathing into whichever mode I find myself in within each moment.

Tell Your Story

What moments in your mothering invite you into a sense of abundance? When do you operate out of a sense of scarcity?

Empty and Full

Artist and spiritual director Melanie Weidner beautifully captures the dynamics of scarcity and abundance in her painting *Fill*. The painting is a series of four images that each feature a clay cup with a deep crack in the side. In the first image, the cup floats in the air, water pours out of its cracked side like a river, and you sense how close to empty the cup is. In the second, water still pours out the side, but water also flows into the top of the cup, indicating a delicate balance of giving and receiving. In the third, the cracked cup sits on the surface of a body of water, and it is unclear whether water pours out or in. And finally, in the fourth image, the cup is submerged in the water, full of water within and without, despite its brokenness.

I believe we live in the last of the four images; we are surrounded by a sea of love, a force field of God's presence. Instead of pouring out love until we are dry or pulling in love until we are full, I believe that we exist within a dynamic sea of love that flows around and through us.

Yet we often find it difficult to experience that reality; we more often feel like we've given and poured out until we have nothing left. I struggle to break from the mind-set that I pour out of myself into my children until I am empty. Weidner's painting calls me to remember that while I am pouring out, my children are pouring in, and the ocean of God's love surrounds us. Somehow, in some way, God's love encompasses us at all times. It is a love that keeps us full.

Tell Your Story

What is it like to consider yourself surrounded by love? How does that influence your experiences of scarcity and abundance, as you and your children pour God's love into one another?

Pain and Gift

Recently I walked through a season of deep compassion, of suffering with and caring for friends and family members who were experiencing profound loss and heartbreak. One day, I visited a chapel, lit candles, and prayed for my loved ones before an icon of Christ on the cross. I touched the wounded feet of Jesus and felt him bear my pain as I bore the pain of my loved ones. I experienced the weight and heartbreak and powerlessness of my compassion, of crying with and suffering with, and I felt the honor of this invitation to co-suffer. Deep compassion draws us into the heart of Christ, who bears all our hurt. It is pain, and it is gift.

I recognized deep compassion as true love: It breaks us open in suffering and awe.

We especially can experience this depth of love in motherhood. Our hearts are intertwined with our children, and when they are hurting—whether from a small scrape or a large and painful loss—we hurt alongside them.

One Sunday morning, I helped care for the two- and three-year-olds at my church, and we went outside to blow bubbles. Healy put the wand of the bubbles she was holding into her mouth, and a teen helper asked her not to. Healy burst into tears, ran to me, threw her sweaty arms around my legs, and buried her tear-streaked face into my lap. It was such a trivial incident, but I could feel every bit of the emotion coursing through her small body: fear about being disciplined by someone she didn't know, shame and guilt at being in trouble. There was nothing small in what her heart experienced.

I held her, and I felt a jolt of empathetic pain in my own heart. But on the heels of that pain came a wave of quiet joy as she calmed in my arms. I could feel the love that courses between mother and daughter. I felt grateful to be in that moment with her and to meet her pain with unwavering compassion.

It is a profound privilege to love as Christ loves.

Tell Your Story

How have you felt the pain of compassion for your children? How has that compassion also felt like gift?

Going and Staying

In that recent season of compassion, I also experienced its limits. While my heart has expanded outward and become more able to welcome and accommodate others' pain, I cannot spend as many days—or sometimes even as many hours—as I want to with those whose suffering I try to help carry. I love my calling to the ministry of presence, and I desire to sit with those I love in their difficulties; but my kids get me first and most. I am both more present and less present, more available and less available. I can give less of my heart and my time despite how much I long to enter fully into the pain of those around me.

This continues to be a holy tension for me. Where do I say: *I need to go. I need to be present to this extraordinary event. I need to be a listening and loving presence to be true to who I am and who God created me to be?* And where do I say: *No, I can't go. I can't be the one to step in because these three beings depend on me for consistency. They need me to hold them and feed them and read to them and tuck them in*

*at night and to provide the mundane, consistent framework
that nurtures their growth?*

When do they sacrifice? When do I sacrifice?

I wish I had a simple equation to follow: I get x number
of hours a week and the kids get y, an easy formula that we
could all understand and follow. Of course, life isn't that
neat, and instead this holy tension invites me into discernment. I notice the needs of my children and my partner,
my own needs, and the needs of my extended circle. I am
drawn into deeper listening, a holy space of attending to the
movements of the Holy Spirit.

The tension of sacrifice draws me into closer relationship. Sometimes the relationship I'm tending means that I
explain to my children why I won't be available to tuck them
in one night. Sometimes I'm drawn into closer relationship
with my children, and I focus my energy on them. Our sacrifices and our choices remind us that we are all image-bear-
ers, and every relationship is holy. On whomever I focus my
attention, I have the chance to see the face of Christ.

Tell Your Story

*How have you had to choose between going and
staying as you've raised your children? How have
these decisions of sacrifice shaped you and led you
deeper into the holiness God is growing in you?*

Yes and No

My deepest sense of myself, my gifts, and my calling is in being a "foul-weather friend." I like to step into the hard spaces of life, to be present in extraordinary times, and to bring the compassion of Christ and the co-suffering of Jesus to others in these times. It feels like a sacrifice when I choose not to accompany others through their pain. Sometimes I do have to make this sacrifice for my children. I have said "no" to attending my sister's birthing of my niece; "no" to visiting family members in the hospital; "no" to so many friends.

Other times I get to say "yes." My husband, parents, in-laws, and friends step in and care for my children so I can be who I am meant to be and serve in the ways I desire to serve. In those moments, each "yes" is a great gift. I sat with my friend's baby girl in the hospital after open-heart surgery and sang to her as she gazed into my eyes with her tiny hand wrapped around my finger. I attended the funeral of another friend's baby boy where we celebrated his beautiful life, mourned his tragic death, and honored my friend's motherhood. I spent time with a friend going through a divorce and wrapped my arms around her as her world fell apart.

When I can be present to someone in pain and suffering, when I can say "yes" instead of "no," I now experience it more deeply. I can be more fully present because I am aware of the gift of the moment and the way my children and others have sacrificed for me to be where I am. In these sacred moments, I feel overwhelmed by the privilege of being with.

We all experience invitations to live into our full self and to use our gifts in a way that takes us away from our children. Whether it is a time to say yes or a time to say no, I hope that it all feels like grace. May you experience the discernment of sacrifice with your children as an opportunity to draw closer to God.

Tell Your Story

When have you been able to say "yes" because others made it possible for you? How has that gift heightened your experience of the moments that come from that "yes"? How do you and your children make sacrifices for one another?

Extraordinary
and Mundane

An intense spring storm brought black clouds that tore open to cascading rain. The storm cleansed the air and the ground and left huge puddles on our city sidewalks.

Declan, Ronan, and Healy begged to go for a "puddle walk," so as soon as we finished dinner, they pulled on their rain boots and hurried outside. The sky was still gray, and the puddles were dark with the mud and dirt that had washed out from the grass. There was nothing particularly beautiful about the evening except for the three children laughing and yelping as they leaped into the puddles and splashed muddy water on their clothes, arms, and faces as they tested how high they could get the water to fly. They wriggled their bodies with joy and made up songs and dances to describe the fun of puddle-splashing.

Ronan noticed me watching them with a smile on my face, and he said, "You're enjoying your children enjoying!"

He could sense the joy and deep awe I felt as I witnessed the glory of their play and the way they made a simple spring day magical. It was extraordinary, and it was made even more so by its fleeting nature. Inside, the table was piled with dirty dishes. Soon I would need to corral my children upstairs for baths and then do laundry to wash the mud off their clothes. I had a headache, and it had been a long Wednesday. In so many ways, it was a typical day. Therein lies the holiness of parenting: The extraordinary is nestled within the mundane; the ordinary holds and highlights the shimmering moments.

If it were all diamonds, they wouldn't sparkle. If my children didn't begin to bicker and whine ten minutes after this joyful moment, it wouldn't have been so sweet. I am grateful for the way the dull, steady rhythm of daily life cradles the moments filled with overwhelming joy.

Tell Your Story

How do you experience the mundane and the extraordinary of motherhood? How does God meet you in each?

More Ourselves and More Like Christ

Take a moment and consider these questions: Who is Jesus to you? How would you describe him? What characteristics define him? Consider the Jesus you meet in scripture and the Christ you meet in prayer. What is he like?

The Jesus I know loves deeply, with force and without condition. He cares for the least of the world. He heals, and he speaks the truth. He breathes mercy. He loves his friends, cares for the crowds, and delights in children. He meets people right where they are.

My best, true self shares many of these qualities. I'm not Jesus, but I am God's beloved child. As I meet myself in my mothering, I also meet the Christ who dwells in me. When my son has been yelling at me and I hold him instead of yelling back; when my daughter asks me to run or dance or roll in the grass with her and I feel awkward but join her in the movement anyway; when I want to read stories to my oldest child but instead create coded messages for him to honor his current greatest love—in these moments, I feel most alive, most myself, and most holy.

I used to think that becoming more holy and becoming more my true self were two separate paths that I could focus on one at a time: I could perform acts of service or I could write; I could read the Bible or I could journal about my desires. But motherhood has taught me that our being is intertwined with God's being. When we focus on ourselves, we encounter our Maker, the God in whom we live and move and have our being. When we focus on God, we cannot escape the lens of ourselves; we can only see God through our own reality.

I love the paradox of this twinning, the inseparability of our identity from God. As we become more ourselves, as we grow into who God has created us to be, we also become more like Christ. The journey of motherhood is a path that leads us into the heart of who we are and into the heart of Christ.

Tell Your Story

How have you become more like Christ when you sought to become more of yourself? How have you become more yourself when you sought to be like Christ? When has this felt like a paradox? When has it felt holy?

Home as Monastery

Sometimes I dream of living in a monastery and sharing life with nuns or monks in a vow of poverty and prayer and community. In monasteries, members have their own rooms for sleeping but share everything else. They cook their meals together and work the land together, and they meet together for set periods of prayer each day. Monastic life seems magical in its simplicity: living outside of culture, sharing life with others, keeping set rhythms of prayer, enjoying simple food and basic but beautiful surroundings, and experiencing ample silence and solitude. In my imagination, it seems almost like a vacation. When I feel like I am just getting by in my cluttered house with my three noisy children, it is hard to imagine an existence less like mine.

Yet over the last few years, I've noticed that parenting is like monastic life in its rhythms and its goals. Motherhood and monasticism require submitting one's will to the spiritual leadership of the community. Just after Declan was born, my husband referred to him as our abbot. It was a joke and a reality as we watched him reorder our days and bend our desires to his needs.

Parenting is monastic in the way it is a life fully integrated. There is no differentiation between work and play, time devoted and time off. There is only life, lived together and with God. At first I railed against this aspect of parenting because I found it impossible to believe that no part of the day or night was mine anymore. Now I recognize the simplicity and holiness of it.

As monastics pray the liturgy of the Hours at fixed points during the day and night, they grow into a life of ceaseless prayer. I would like my ceaseless parenting to become ceaseless prayer. I'm learning to recognize the graces of this season of life as the Holy Order of Burdette. As I embrace a monastic ordering of family life, I wonder what elements I need to include in our family's rule of life, and I try to make commitments to healthful and holy practices: sleep, exercise, quiet time to center in God, space to journal, time to play with one another, time to connect with friends and extended family, and time to read. These are the simple practices that help me be present to this holy life.

Tell Your Story

Take time to play with the idea of the monastic nature of parenting. What does that idea stir up for you? What rhythms or practices do you desire to include in your days and weeks?

This Life That Is Ours

One gray middle-of-the-week morning, my three children played together in my daughter's bedroom. I sat on the floor and let their joy and laughter wash over me. I felt fully alive, present, and grateful. I thought, *This is as good as it gets.* It won't get better at the weekend or better in a year or two.

I want to savor each holy moment and let them determine the rhythm of my life. Instead of weekdays and weekends or work and rest, my life is measured by moments when I am present or not present, flowing or frustrated, open or closed. I prayed: *Lord, teach me how to be in the right posture toward my children, to be open, loving, present, flexible. Teach me to flow like you. Help me to recognize and to pause and to savor these holy moments.* Five minutes later, chaos and bickering once again reigned. That's okay. I'm learning to be present to each moment as it comes instead of wishing away my life.

I experienced a similar moment when we visited our local urban farm. It includes fields of vegetables, an orchard, a bioshelter, and beehives. It is holy ground. My family enjoys the magic of a small labyrinth that winds through an herb garden. Its stone pathway is a physical symbol of the spiritual journey, and it offers a moment of quiet in the usual busyness of the farm. On Good Friday, the seven last words of Jesus were posted around the labyrinth for self-guided reflection. I moved slowly through the labyrinth as I stopped at each sign to be present with Jesus on his journey to the cross and in his death. My children ran around me and through the labyrinth, skipped on and off the path, laughed and danced, and stopped only to pick and taste their favorite herbs.

"Mommy, have you had the orange fennel yet?"

"Mommy, you've got to try the mint. It's delicious!"

Never mind that we're at the farm nearly every week, tasting these same herbs. Never mind my slow, reverent pace. I felt annoyed at their distractions and delighted at their ability to make every small, mundane thing new again. Mostly, I felt both peace and wonder. I thought: *This is the journey. I am moving slowly around the labyrinth of life, and my children are flitting around me, fast and spinning, sometimes on my same path, sometimes not, and it all belongs. Everything is holy.*

I am learning how to be in—and to embrace—this life that is ours.

Tell Your Story

What does it mean for you to embrace the life that is yours? How are you experiencing the presence of God, right where you are?

A PRACTICE TO SUSTAIN YOU

For many years, Nick and I were part of the House of Saint Michael, a small community committed to studying the early church mothers and fathers. Members made annual personal commitments to deepen in relationship with Christ in the coming year. One year my friend Eileen, who had recently welcomed her first child, said, "I commit to an Examen of Motherhood. I will try to reflect each day on the ways God has been present to me through my daughter and the ways God has been distant."

Eileen's words sent shivers down my spine as the full, holy potential of her commitment opened before me. As a spiritual director, I was intimately familiar with the Examen. The Examen helps you explore the movements of the day to notice where you have felt most alive and where God has felt most present and most absent. The difficult moments may prompt you to seek forgiveness. It closes with turning your attention to the day to come and asking God for graces you may need, such as patience or strength or wisdom.

In this book, we have been exploring how to experience God's presence in our mothering by learning a variety of ways to notice the holiness of our work and the Holy Spirit's movement through it. The Examen can help foster further awareness of God in your mothering each day. Its structure can help you to make this noticing habitual.

That word *noticing* is particularly important. The Examen is a tool of naming. It is not a tool of judgment. As we reflect on our time with our children, our natural inclination is to think about what we did right or wrong in our parenting. We can easily slip into self-criticism when we look at our days on our own. By instead asking God to look at our days with us, we begin to see as God sees. Praying the Examen is about noticing the reality of what has happened and growing in relationship with the God of Things as They Are.

To help you quiet the judgment that may run through your head, begin by asking God to guide your time. You might pray, *God, take me back through this day and help me see what you would have me see* or *God, may this time be yours.* Find your own way to ground your time in God.

Then enter the prayer of noticing. Here is an example Examen of Motherhood, which I encourage you to pray slowly, quietly, and with time for reflection:

> *Recall your time with your children today. What moments were full of joy and light? When did you notice God's presence? Savor these life-giving moments. What moments were hardest, dry and empty, overwhelming and exhausting? What might God be saying to you as you reflect on this day with your children? What invitation are you hearing? Finally, turn your attention to the day to come.*

What does the future hold for you? What grace do you need for what is ahead?

Praying the Examen helps us to notice patterns throughout our days. Over time, as you practice the Examen of Motherhood, I invite you to consider the following: What helps you move toward greater life, love, and freedom? How are you becoming more fully yourself? What moves you toward self-protection or smallness? When does God feel distant? How do you sense the holy?

I hope the Examen of Motherhood helps you create space to sit and be alone with yourself and with God. The Examen can flow naturally into a time of silent prayer. Silence lets the events and thoughts from the day sift through you. The insignificant events fall away, while moments that seemed trivial bubble up and unveil their meaning. Held by your loving, curious gaze, they reveal glimmers of God's presence.

I hope you also find physical practices that help you care for your body and honor the tangible work of motherhood. Light a candle with an evocative scent. Drink from a special mug that fits in your hand just right. Massage lotion into your hands after you wash them. Walk around the block to experience fresh air. Do gentle yoga. Run. Take a warm bath. As you engage in these practices, thank God for the gift of your body, and let God thank you for all that you do.

Above all, I pray that you find practices that help you to be more present to the moment-by-moment sacredness of your mothering. It is holy work.

A CLOSING WORD

I have been working on this book for years, and I am still living into its questions. I continue to wonder each day how God is moving in my children, in me, and in our lives together. I suspect I will be living these questions my whole life. Some days God feels so present, tangible, and awe-inspiring, I can feel the hairs stand up on my arms in response. Other days I am dry, tired, and feel dead inside. I am still learning to experience both days with peace and an open heart.

On a recent retreat, I asked God, *How do I really know you are present? How can I trust this path you've set before me?* I posed the question in a stunning chapel, surrounded by rainbow-colored stained glass and the light pouring through its panes.

God answered me in the light. I felt the presence of the Holy Spirit wrap around me and flow through me. God was in the bands of colorful light, swirling around and holding me. It was a moment beyond words. When I feel dry and alone, I return to this memory to be held and refreshed, to experience again the Holy Spirit mothering me, wrapping around me, and creating me anew. I experienced God's presence in the light, not despite my mothering but because of it. I know God's love as Creator in ways I did not experience before becoming a mother.

Together we have explored motherhood and turned a kaleidoscope to view its myriad, mysterious, holy facets. You have walked your own sacred journey through this book and experimented with frameworks to support you as you live into these questions. I leave you now with this image of the Holy Spirit swirling around you and moving through you as bands of light that hold and love and refresh you. May this image birth your own sacred images of the journey of motherhood. May your mothering reveal to you new layers of the mystery of God's love.

We close with a blessing:

May you have time to savor the holiness of your
     mothering,
To sink into this sacred calling,
To experience your hands as caring for Christ
As you care for your children.
May you continue to awaken to the beauty of your
     family and the beauty of yourself.
May you become more fully yourself and more fully
     like Christ.
May you dance with the chaos.
May your path unfold before you.
May you experience the divine within you,
     breathing deeply,
This day and every day.
Amen.

NOTES

Introduction

1. Kahlil Gibran, *The Broken Wings,* trans. Anthony R. Ferris (New York: The Citadel Press, 1957), 92.
2. Thomas Merton, *Conjectures of a Guilty Bystander* (New York: Image, 2009), 153–55.

Preparation Days

1. John O'Donohue, *To Bless the Space Between Us* (New York: Doubleday, 2008), 15.
2. Walter J. Burghardt, SJ, *Seasons That Laugh or Weep: Musings on the Human Journey* (New York/Ramsey: Paulist Press, 1983), 103.

Ego Deaths

1. Lisa Miller, PhD, *The Spiritual Child: The New Science on Parenting for Health and Lifelong Thriving* (New York: Picador, 2015), 318.

Beholding Beauty

1. Jan L. Richardson, *In the Sanctuary of Women: A Companion for Reflection and Prayer* (Nashville: Upper Room Books, 2010), 38.
2. Krista Tippett, *Becoming Wise: An Inquiry into the Mystery and Art of Living* (New York: Penguin Press, 2016), 75.